SERMONS FOR THE TIMES

by

Henry Clay Morrison

First Fruits Press
Wilmore, Kentucky
c2012

asburyseminary.edu
800.2ASBURY
204 North Lexington Avenue
Wilmore, Kentucky 40390

First Fruits
THE ACADEMIC OPEN PRESS OF ASBURY SEMINARY

ISBN: 9780984738649

Sermons for the Times, by H.C. Morrison.
First Fruits Press, © 2012
Pentecostal Publishing Company, © 1921

Digital version at http://place.asburyseminary.edu/firstfruitsheritagematerial/5/

First Fruits Press
B.L. Fisher Library
Asbury Theological Seminary
204 N. Lexington Ave.
Wilmore, KY 40390
http://place.asburyseminary.edu/firstfruits

Morrison, H. C. (Henry Clay), 1857-1942.
  Sermons for the times / by H.C. Morrison.
  Wilmore, Ky. : First Fruits Press, c2012.
  138 p. ; 21 cm.
  Reprint. Previously published: Previously published: Louisville, Ky. :
  Pentecostal Publishing Company, c1921.
  ISBN: 9780984738649 (pbk.)
  1. Sermons, American. 2. Methodist Church—Sermons.. I. Title.
BX833 .M6 S4 2012

Cover design by Haley Hill

asburyseminary.edu
800.2ASBURY
204 North Lexington Avenue
Wilmore, Kentucky 40390

First Fruits
THE ACADEMIC OPEN PRESS OF ASBURY SEMINARY

SERMONS FOR THE TIMES

BY

REV. H. C. MORRISON, D. D.

PENTECOSTAL PUBLISHING COMPANY.
Louisville, Ky.

DEDICATION.

This book of sermons is affectionately dedicated to my wife who, with her faithful typewriter, and in many other ways, rendered me great assistance in its preparation.

H. C. MORRISON.

FOREWORD.

This winter, while kept out of the pulpit by illness, I determined to speak, as far as possible, through the press to the people in the form of a series of practical sermons. The sermons contained herein are not doctrinal, but as indicated by the title, "Sermons for the Times." I have a conviction that there is great need for just such proclamation of truth as is herein contained.

A few days ago, after the book was set up, proved and ready for the press, I fell upon an address signed by all of the Bishops of the M. E. Church, South. I clipped from that address a few paragraphs which I believe to be startlingly true, the substance of which was in my mind in the writing of the following sermons, and is my apology for sending out this book to the public.

"We have fallen on troublesome times. The whole world is turned upside down. Waves of crime are sweeping over our beloved country. Disregard of the Christian Sabbath and indifference to the sanctity of marriage have become distressingly common among our American people. Even many church members have become 'lovers of pleasure more than lovers of God.' Selfishness reigns in all departments of life—in the dealings of capital with labor and in the dealings of labor with capital.

"There is but one hope for America—in the religion of our Lord and Saviour Jesus Christ. For there is no foundation for prosperity either national or individual, except in morality; and there is no sure foundation for morality except in religion. Without religion morality has no compelling sanctions, and no sufficient dynamic.

"Forty years ago Christlieb, a great German preacher, warned his countrymen that their Kultur was separating itself from the Christian religion and, if not checked, would plunge Germany into the abyss. His prophetic warning was not heeded. Germany plunged into the abyss and came near wrecking the whole world.

"Let America be warned. Philosophy, science, and even religion have in most of our American universities gone far astray from the principles and practices which have made America great as a nation. The greatest menace to our Republic just now is moral and spiritual bankruptcy."

The only hope for the nation is in the religion of the Lord Jesus and warning of this fact must be brought home to the people by an earnest and powerful appeal from the ministry. We must return to faith in the Bible, to the fear of God, to the great doctrine of the New Birth. We must insist that the individual be born again; the people must be brought to hate sin and to love holiness.   Faithfully,

H. C. MORRISON.

CONTENTS.

THE RESPONSIBILITY OF THE MINISTRY

"Because with lies ye have made the heart of the righteous sad, whom I have not made sad; and strengthened the hands of the wicked, that he should not return from his wicked ways, by promising him life: therefore, ye shall see no more vanity, nor divine divinations: for I will deliver my people out of your hand: and ye shall know that I am the Lord."—Ezek. 13:22, 23.

Much of the early part of the prophecy of Ezekiel is a message from God to the prophets themselves. God is instructing, encouraging, and warning His messengers to the people. In the second chapter of this revelation Ezekiel himself receives most positive and specific instruction with reference to his mission and message. He is notified that he is sent to a rebellious nation, an impudent people. He is instructed that he is not to fear the people, even if he is rejected and suffers severe persecution. "Be not

9

afraid of their words, nor be dismayed at their looks. And thou shalt say unto them, 'Thus saith the Lord God.' And they, whether they will hear, or whether they will forbear (for they are a rebellious house), yet shall they know that there has been a prophet among them."

I cannot conceive of stronger, clearer, and more authoritative instruction from God to one of His messengers than these words to Ezekiel. "Fear them not;" suffer, if you must, give them your message as received from me; tell them, "Thus saith the Lord," and whatever they may do with the message, or however they may persecute and afflict you, yet they shall be compelled to admit in their own hearts, that you are the Lord's prophet.

There are further very specific instructions to Ezekiel that should be quoted as it came direct from God: "Son of man, I have made thee a watchman unto the house of Israel: therefore hear the word at my mouth, and give them warning from me. When I say unto the wicked, Thou shalt surely die; and thou givest him not warning, nor speakest to warn the wicked from his wicked way, to save his life; the same wicked man shall die in his iniquity; but his blood will I require at thine hand. Yet if thou warn the wicked, and he turn not from his wickedness, nor from his wicked way, he shall die in his iniquity; but thou hast delivered thy soul."

"Again, when a righteous man doth turn from his righteousness, and commit iniquity, and I lay a stumbling block before him, he shall die: because thou hast not given him warning, he shall die in his sin, and his righteousness which he hath done shall not be remembered; but his blood will I require at thine hand. Nevertheless if thou warn the righteous man, that the righteous sin not, and he doth not sin, he shall surely live, because he is warned; also thou hast delivered thy soul."

We have quoted at length here, as no thought we could conceive or words we could utter, could convey the great truth of the responsibility that rests upon the prophet of the Lord—the minister of the message of God to the people—so forcibly as these strong words to Ezekiel. We are taught here that God holds the ministers of His truth to strict accountability to Him for the manner in which they proclaim His message. The people may hear or forbear, as they choose, but the salvation of the preacher depends upon his loyalty to God, and the clearness and honesty with which he delivers his message.

The messenger is not held responsible for the effect of his message, or for the manner in which the people spoken to receive it; but he is held responsible for its faithful delivery. It must be noted that his own salvation depends upon his loyalty to the word of the Lord. There is a most solemn warning here that no prophet of olden or modern times can afford to ignore. If the messenger fails to deliver the truth of God as received from Him, the wicked or the backslidden may die in their sins, but their blood will be required at the hands of the messenger who fails to discharge his solemn duty in giving the people the word of the Lord.

It should be noted here that the messenger of God is to warn the people. He is to speak to them faithfully with reference to the importance of obedience to the divine word. He must rebuke them for their sins. He must point them faithfully to the inevitable results that must follow upon disobedience to the divine commandments. He must thunder the law of God into their ears. He must stand firmly and fearlessly for divine truth whether the people will hear or whether they will forbear.

Let it be borne in mind that the God of the Bible never changes. He is the same yesterday, today and forever. He alone can call, commission, and send forth His messengers. There could be nothing more presumptuous or sinful than that a man in any ecclesiastical position whatsoever, should undertake to usurp the place of God, and presume to select, call, and commission and send forth prophets to proclaim the message of the Lord. God has reserved unto Himself this high prerogative. He alone can call and commission the ministers of His word; and He will call them into judgment if they fail to be true to their commission. The messengers of the Lord must report to their divine Master.

Nothing could be more unscriptural, impudent, and presumptuous, than for a man uncalled of God to assume the role of preacher. It is equally rash and dangerous for a man called of God to turn away from the word of the Lord, and instead of giving the people the Lord's message, to give his own opinions, notions, theories or philosophies in contradiction of the word of God, and thus betray his trust, lead the people astray, delude their souls, let them perish in their sins, and at last appear at the judgment seat with their blood upon him.

The Protestant Church has no more authority or power to call men into the ministry than the Roman Catholic Church has to forgive men their sins. The Church, if wholly consecrated to Christ, separate from the world, and filled with the Holy Spirit, can travail in prayer, call down revival power, and bring forth sons and daughters born of the Holy Ghost, and from among them thus "born again" God will call His ministers, mis-

sionaries, and messengers, and they must
get their message from the mouth of the
Lord.

We can conceive of the Church drift-
ing from the channels of truth, becoming
lukewarm in her love, careless in her
obedience, worldly in her heart and backslidden in her life, so that there become
"a famine of the word of God," and her
pulpits become empty. There is a scarcity of ministers; the Macedonian call for
help from the mission field goes un-
heeded, and then we can conceive of the
Church, instead of becoming penitent,
waiting before the Lord in fasting and
prayer, and hungering and thirsting after
righteousness, calling upon God for the
return of His grace and mercy, and seeking for that spiritual awakening and religious revival which will bring sons and
daughters into the kingdom, born of the
travail of Zion, begotten of the Holy
Spirit, and fitted for the choosing and
sending forth of God as His messengers.
We say, we can conceive of the Church
in a lukewarm and backslidden state with
a scarcity of preachers and missionaries,

instead of returning to the Lord, under-
taking to take His place and select His
messengers; going out, and persuading,
promising and inducing young people to
volunteer their services upon a God they
do not know, whose voice they have never
heard, and whose message they cannot
bear to the people.

In this 13th chapter of Ezekiel, from
which we get our text, God has a contro-
versy with prophets who have not remained true to His word.   He says they
have "daubed with untempered mortar,"
and their walls will fall.   The figure is a
very suggestive one.   A wall may be high,
symmetrical, and beautiful, but if the
cement used is not such as will hold fast
in rains, freezes, and all sorts of atmos-
pheric tests, the wall must fall.   Just so,
with all preaching and religious teaching;
if it is not founded on the word of God
and cemented with His truth, in times of
testing it will fall into utter ruin, and in
the day of judgment it will be found to
be only frail, human rubbish instead of
the abiding and eternal truth of God.   It
is only the word of the Lord that abideth

forever. The heavens and the earth may pass away, but the word of the Lord cannot pass or change. It will abide through the ceaseless cycles of eternity.

In the text a fearful accusation is brought against the delinquent and unfaithful prophet. "Thou hast made the heart of the righteous sad, whom I have not made sad; and strengthened the hands of the wicked, that he should not return from his wicked ways, by promising him life." The message these prophets were delivering was not the message of the Lord; they were the fictions and imaginations of their own backslidden hearts. These false teachers grieved the hearts of the Lord's people and comforted the wicked in their rebellion. God serves notice upon these prophets that He will punish them and deliver His people out of their hands.

This text, with its message, is remarkably applicable to conditions existing in our nation at the present time. The destructive critics in a number of the theological schools of this country, in many pulpits, and through the press in

their attacks upon the inspiration of the
Word of God, are saddening the hearts of
true Christians everywhere, and are comforting the wicked and strengthening
their hands in their sins. These false
teachers are sending forth no earnest plea
for faithfulness to the holy oracles of the
Lord, no solemn warning and call to repentance to those who are trampling
upon the divine commandments. They
grieve the souls of the righteous with their
false teaching and then mock their grief
by accusing them of ignorance, of nar-
rowness, and of failure to keep abreast
with the progressive thought of the times;
meanwhile, they break down the barriers
which God has erected against the rising
tides of sin and turn the flood of wickedness loose upon the world, until there
rises an inundation of crime, of lewdness,
of divorce, of Sabbath desecration, of
unbelief, of unrestrained lust, of covet-
ousness, a mad race for money and wild
and reckless chase for godless pleasure.

These same destructive critics, if per-
mitted to go unrebuked and unchecked,
will bring upon this nation the spiritual

dearth and moral decay and ruin which the same teachers, with the same spirit, and the same perversions of truth, have brought upon Germany. The false teaching might not head up in the same way; it might not be a world war of blood and fire, slaughter, starvation, and human agony, but the sowing of the same seed will produce the same harvest in spiritual and moral effects. The ripened fruit will be the same. A nation that has flung away the Bible, forsaken God and challenged His judgments, will, in the end, suffer the fearful consequence of a people who, having refused to obey the divine commandments and rejected the divine mercy, has nothing left it but the divine wrath.

There is a great army of false teachers going to and fro in this nation today, calling the people through their teachings to many false gods, grieving the hearts of the righteous and giving comfort to the deluded souls of the wicked. Take, for instance, Mormonism, Russellism, and Eddyism; armies of the representatives of these unscriptural cults, both by mouth and through the press, are going about everywhere, zealously sowing the seeds of a false propaganda. Mark you, they are not calling the people to repentance, they are not warning sinners to flee from the wrath to come, they are not entreating wicked men to seek the Lord Jesus Christ in His pardoning mercy, but they are scattering broadcast teachings in direct contradiction to the truths of the Holy Bible; they are "grieving the hearts of the righteous, and strengthening the hands of the wicked." Some of them are promising the possibility of reformation and repentance in a future state; some of them are substituting the word of God with a human jumble of contradictions of the Holy Bible which contains neither reason nor righteousness; some of them are denying that there is any such thing as sin, or person as Satan, or place as hell. All of them are comforting the hearts of the impenitent wicked in their sins and promising them life without true repentance and saving faith in the Lord Jesus Christ.

There is a revival of Unitarianism in

this nation; not so much, perhaps, in the Unitarian Church, as in the sowing of their seeds of thought and false teaching into evangelical congregations; and it comes to pass that not a few ministers, boasting of their own generosity of spirit and breadth of view, are offering salvation very nearly on the same plane upon which it is offered by Unitarian preachers themselves: i. e., salvation without faith in Christ and the atonement which He made upon Calvary. Not a few Protestant ministers in the looseness of their theology and their boasted broadness, which amounts to infidelity to Jesus Christ, will recognize as Christian brethren men who deny the deity of our Lord and refuse to partake of the sacrament, that last supper, which He established on the evening before His arrest, and commanded His Church to keep through the ages. We are far from recommending a spirit of hatred toward any man; we insist upon the spirit of love for all men, but we cannot recognize men as brethren in our Lord who deny the deity of Jesus and offer their fellow-beings salvation without faith in His all-atoning blood.

These same Protestant preachers who boast of their liberal views and their broad generosity, many of them, are teaching upon a plane but little, if anything above, the Universalist. Not a few of them are intimating that, in the end, all men will be saved, whatever their lives may have been, regardless of the fact that they lived and died in their sins. All of this host of false teachers come within the limit and under the censure and condemnation of the teachings of our text. "They make the hearts of the righteous sad; they strengthen the hands of the wicked by promising them life."

The Lord Jesus Christ has said, "Except a man be born again he cannot see the kingdom of God." We fear, not a few evangelists of our time are substituting for this mysterious and gracious work of the Holy Spirit, by which a man is made in Christ a new creature, a mere "profession of faith," a "hitting the trail," or some human act, which by no means gives the actor a new heart devoted to the love and service of the Lord Jesus Christ. We are quite certain that thousands of children have been brought into the Church on "Decision Day" without any sort of true conception of evangelical repentance, or heart experience of sins forgiven and the regenerating power of the Spirit of God. Such people will grow up to antagonize genuine religious experience of which they know nothing, and they will become the easy victims and followers of all sorts of false teachers. They, with their sympathy and money, will encourage and support the destructive critics; they will furnish a following for Eddyism, Russellism, and the various false teachings and human philosophies which, under the shrewd devices of Satan, take the place of the Gospel of the Lord Jesus, which is the power of God unto salvation. They will rally around the standards of those easy-going and popular preachers of the day who promise men life on a low plane without denying self, seeking a new heart, taking up the cross and following the Christ.

We do not desire or intend to become

an accuser of our brethren, but is it not true that in many pulpits of today there is no strong voice against worldliness, no mighty outcry against the popular sins which sweep the people away from the Bible, its solemn warnings, its majestic laws, and its saving gospel?

It must be admitted by all serious and thoughtful people, that there are not a few men in high places in the churches who are seeking by various methods of mental-moral training, to substitute the regenerating work of the Holy Ghost and the earnest preaching of the gospel for the salvation of men. They are insinuating that there is no special need of a great spiritual crisis—namely, the new birth. They are telling us that men are born in a state of moral purity; that all they need is favorable conditions, proper surroundings, and moral instruction. Thus, they would set aside the work of the Holy Ghost, the power of the gospel, and replace the divine plan with mere human teachings and substitutes. These men have much to say about the natural purity of the babe, the importance of environ-

ment, the uplift of education.   They
utterly fail to emphasize human depravity, the necessity of an atonement, the
need of regeneration, and thus they are
bringing into the Church a host of unregenerated people, grieving the hearts of
the righteous, and strengthening the
hands of those who have no experimental
knowledge of the Lord Jesus Christ as a
personal Savior.

The world war brought to light the
fact that we have a host of preachers in
the supposedly evangelical churches of
this nation, who have so far drifted away
from the word of God that they went up
and down the land teaching that soldiers
who gave themselves to die upon the
battlefield in a righteous cause, made for
themselves a sacrifice sufficient to atone
for their sins.   This teaching was common and widespread.   I heard it proclaimed with my own ears to a large
number of soldiers from one of the most
popular pulpits in the state of Kentucky.
These deceivers of the people who have
drifted away from the truth of God would
send our boys reeking in their sins to the

battle charge, trusting in their own deeds and blood, in the awful moment of death, instead of turning their eyes and lifting their prayers to the blessed Christ, who gave Himself a ransom for sinners, and who has said, "Whosoever cometh unto me, I will in no wise cast out." The impudence of these false teachers, when their attention was called to the danger of offering men salvation apart from the Lord Jesus, was bold and insolent. The war did not make these men what they were, but it gave them an opportunity to speak out the unbelief in their hearts; and while they may not be so reckless in times of peace, as they were under the stress and excitement of the war, nevertheless the signing of the Armistice did not change their unbelieving hearts; they are the same today—"Blind leaders of the blind"—saddening the hearts of the righteous and strengthening the hands of the wicked.

This doctrine of atoning for one's sins by giving one's life upon the battlefield is no new doctrine. It has been taught by the bloody Mohammedans through

the centuries.   Heathen peoples who
knew nothing of the Bible and the Christ
have stirred their soldiers to heroic deeds
by promising them a future of peace and
glory, provided they met death at the
hands of their enemies on the field of
carnage.   How contrary the teaching of
these heathen philosophers and chief-
tains, and backslidden, false teachers in
the churches of this country, to the
teachings of the Holy Scriptures.   The
keynote of the gospel is, "For by grace
are ye saved through faith; and that not
of yourselves; it is the gift of God; not
of works, lest any man should boast." The
great apostle Paul in speaking of our
Lord Jesus, declared, "Neither is there
salvation in any other: for there is none
other name under heaven given among
men, whereby we must be saved." Our
Lord Himself says, "I am the door: he
that entereth not by the door into the
sheepfold, but climbeth up some other
way, the same is a thief and a robber."
The whole Bible, in all of its teachings
with reference to human salvation, in
Old Testament and New, gathers about

this one great truth which is the central
sun of the entire Christian system, that
in Christ alone there is redemption, forgiveness of sins, the sanctifying of the
nature and everlasting life.

Yet, in the face of the whole of the inspired teaching, scores of men in popular
pulpits have been offering salvation to the
soldiers if they gave their lives for others;
and that almost without challenge or
objection from their congregations or the
Christian public. Why should not these
false teachers enlarge upon their new
scheme of human redemption entirely
outside of the Lord Jesus, by claiming
that the mother who gives her life for her
babe, by that act saves herself; the wicked
fireman who is killed by a falling wall,
trying to rescue some one from a burning
building, by that act saves himself; that
the farmer who is laboring for the support of his family, caught out in a rain,
taking cold and dying of pneumonia, has
atoned for his sins by his labors and ex-
posures for his household, and thus, shut
Christ entirely out and let men save
themselves by their sacrifice for their

fellow-beings. The simple truth is, there
is very much religious teaching along
these lines in this country without any
sort of scriptural warrant, and in most
positive contradiction to the teachings of
the Lord Jesus and His apostles.   These
false teachers come clearly under the
sentence pronounced in our text: "They
sadden the hearts of the righteous, they
strengthen the hands of the wicked," and
they will appear at the judgment bar with
the blood of the souls they have deluded
upon their skirts.

It is impossible to contemplate the line
of thought suggested by our text without
thinking of the deluded millions of
people under the influence of Romanism,
with its towering temples, tinseled altars,
dim lights, mumbling priests and splendid pageantry of worship, promising
pardon, praying for the dead, offering
life to the living, proposing to rescue
those who have died in their sins from
purgatorial fires, and teaching the people
to look for life and salvation through the
jugglery of the priesthood of an apostate
church instead of forsaking sin and trust-

ing alone in the cleansing blood of a crucified Christ.

But the subject grows upon us; the heart becomes sick and weary with the contemplation. Truly, we are living in perilous times, "There is a famine of the word of God." The Bible plainly declares that, "Without holiness no man shall see the Lord." Jesus was manifested to destroy the works of the devil, to restore man to communion and fellowship with the eternal Father by separating man from that which had separated him from the Father—*sin.*

The great end and aim of the atonement is the destruction of sin, the purifying of man, his restoration to his original state of holiness, harmony and co-operation with God. "The blood of Jesus Christ His Son cleanseth us from all sin." This is the great message of the ministry, the great object and desire of the eternal Father, the reason why He gave His Son to die upon the cross. This is the keynote of the gospel—salvation in Jesus, salvation from sin, restoration to holiness, communion and harmony with God.

O, that these great truths might be proclaimed throughout the world, that the mouths of the deceivers of the people might be silenced, that all men standing in the pulpits of this great country, with one accord would lift up their voices against the sins of the people, the crying evils of the times, faithfully and fearlessly warn men of judgment to come, and whether the people will hear or forbear, let them know that the prophets of the Lord are among them and thus save their own souls.

The closing verse of this text speaks of coming judgment. God declares that He will deliver His people out of the hands of their false teachers. By and by, His judgments will come so fearful, that the people will be made to realize that they are from God; that they will be made to see their own wickedness, to discover that their religious teachers are untrue to God and to them; calamities will fall upon nations and people who follow the leadership of false prophets. The judgments of the Lord must follow the violation of His laws. No greater calamity can befall a nation than that the men who stand up in the pulpits claiming to be the messengers of the Lord, should be untrue to the word of God, unfaithful in their warnings and admonitions, unscriptural and deceptive in their teachings; in the end, it means judgment and destruction.

Give a nation a faithful ministry in its pulpits, men who feel the call and awe of God upon them; men who will be true to His word, declare His truth regardless of consequences, who will faithfully instruct men in righteousness and warn them against sin; men who will rebuke wickedness among the rich as well as the poor, who making the word of the Lord the sword of the Spirit, will strike mightily against the sins of the people and warn them of judgment to come, meanwhile, with tender and loving heart, calling them to repentance and pointing them to the Lamb of God who taketh away the sin of the world. Such a nation can but be blessed. There will be power in the churches; the fires of devotion will glow

upon millions of family altars; there will
be order and happiness in the home; the
schools will be centers of spiritual and
intellectual development; there will be
honesty in commerce, justice in the
courts, civic righteousness will prevail,
moral standards will be high, social life
will be pure, the fear of God will pervade
the earth, the love of Christ will reign and
rule in the hearts of men, the Bible will
become the revered and honored book,
and the kingdom of heaven will be set up
in the hearts of the people; and our
crucified and risen Lord "shall see of the
travail of His soul, and shall be satisfied."

THE CHURCH THE BRIDE OF CHRIST

"And now if ye will deal kindly and truly with my master, tell me: and if not, tell me; that I may turn to the right hand, or to the left."

Sarah, the wife of Abraham, had died. The tent was empty and desolate; the father and son were sad. There is no home so empty as that out of which a good wife and mother has gone to return no more. In his meditations Abraham was reminded that Isaac was of marriageable age. He also recalled the fact that the promise was that, "In Isaac shall thy seed be blessed." Isaac was to be the father of a great nation, therefore, Isaac's wife must be the mother of the family from which the nation should spring.

No doubt, Abraham meditated upon the fact that you cannot have a good family without a good mother. This seems to be a universal rule. Not infrequently children are a large improvement upon

34

their father. We have known some excellent families of children whose fathers were wicked, drunken and worthless; but their mothers were the handmaidens of the Lord; their prayers and faith overcame the evil influences of a godless father and they were able to train up their children in sobriety, lead them to Christ in their youth, and build up, by the grace and help of God, devout and excellent families.

The mother's influence in the family is so close and intimate, so far-reaching and effective, that if she be a godly and devout woman the impress upon her children is most likely to be good and abiding. We can hardly hope for an excellent and devout family of children who are the offspring, under the early influence and guidance of a godless, gad-about and worthless mother.

Abraham was determined that Isaac should not take for wife any of the women of the mixed and mongrel breeds of the people of the land in which he dwelt; for this reason he called unto him Eliezer, his chief servant, a faithful and trusted

man, and had him to place his hand
under his thigh, an ancient Eastern cus-
tom, and take a solemn oath that he
would not take a wife unto Isaac of the
daughters of the Canaanites, but that he
would go to Abraham's country and
kindred to find a bride for Isaac.

Having taken the oath the servant took
ten camels of his master and with his
retinue of servants departed and went to
Mesopotamia and came to the city of
Nahor. It was here that he lifted up his
heart to God in prayer that the damsel
who should come to the well, to whom he
should say, "Let down thy pitcher, I pray
thee, that I may drink; and she shall
say, Drink, and I will give thy camels
drink also: let the same be she that thou
hast appointed for thy servant Isaac; and
thereby shall I know that thou hast
showed kindness unto my master."

The servant had hardly done praying
until Rebekah, a beautiful damsel, came
tripping to the well. In the providence
of God, it turned out that she was of
Abraham's household; perhaps a second
cousin of Isaac's. The scriptures say she

was "Very fair to look upon." No sooner
had Abraham's servant asked her for
drink than she hasted to offer him drink
and also to draw water for his camels,
thus, fitting perfectly in answer to the
prayer the servant had just offered to the
Lord.

Eliezer was so delighted that he at once
gave her "a golden earring of a half
shekel weight, and two bracelets for her
hands of ten shekels weight of gold."
Rebekah assured Eliezer that he would
be welcome to her home, that there was
straw and provender for his beasts and
room to lodge. Abraham's servant was
filled with gratitude and blessed the Lord
for His guiding hand. Rebekah hastened
into the house and told her mother and
her brother Laban of her experience at
the well, and showed them the beautiful
gifts that Abraham's servant had be-
stowed upon her.

Then Laban came out and invited
Eliezer to come into the house, and to
bring in his beasts. The invitation was
gratefully accepted; the camels were
ungirded, straw and provender were pro-

vided, water was furnished for the washing of his feet, and for the washing of the men's feet who were with him. A table was spread for his refreshment and he was invited to partake. But Eliezer burdened with his message and mission, said "I will not eat until I have told my errand." He revealed his identity, related the story of Abraham and his great wealth. He told of the death of Sarah, his master's wife, and how he had been commissioned to find a bride for Isaac, and how that he had prayed for divine guidance and had been led of the hand of the Lord. He related also, the prayer he had offered to the Lord for a sign at the well, and how the coming and conduct of Rebekah had fitted perfectly into the request he had made of the Lord. And then he said to the family in the language of text, "If ye will deal kindly and truly with my master: tell me: and if not, tell me; that I may turn to the right hand, or to the left."

The father and brother of Rebekah answered, "The thing proceedeth from the Lord: we cannot speak unto thee bad or good. Behold, Rebekah is before thee, take her, and go, and let her be thy master's son's wife, as the Lord hath spoken." This decision of Rebekah's family brought great joy to the heart of Eliezer, and immediately he opened his treasures and brought forth beautiful presents of jewels, gold and silver, and raiment, and gave them to Rebekah, and he also gave to her brother and her mother precious things.

It was a time of feasting and joy in the home of Bethuel; in the morning Laban and his mother entreated Abraham's servant to permit Rebekah to remain with them for a time, at least ten days, and after that she should take her journey to Isaac. But Eliezer refused to remain, and insisted that he return at once to his master with Rebekah. The damsel was called and the matter was left with her. "Wilt thou go with this man? And she said, I will go." Thus the matter was settled and Eliezer, with his train of camels, his servants, and the old nurse of Rebekah, took their departure with the blessing of Rebekah's family.

As the caravan approached Abraham's country, "Isaac went out to meditate in the field at eventide: and he lifted up his eyes, and saw, and behold, the camels were coming." Abraham's servant seeing his young master told Rebekah it was Isaac, and thus he brought Rebekah to his young master, and the record says, "Isaac brought her into his mother, Sarah's tent, and took Rebekah and she became his wife; and he loved her: and Isaac was comforted after the death of his mother."

There is a deep and significant spiritual interpretation of this beautiful romance in the early history of the Hebrew people. In the interpretation of this romance we see in Abraham a type of the infinite Father; Isaac is a beautiful type of our Lord Jesus, and Eliezer represents the minister of the gospel filled with the Holy Ghost, and under solemn oath and guidance of the Spirit, to go out and find a bride for Christ. Let it be noted here that Abraham's servant was not to find a bride for Isaac among the heathen peoples about him, but was to return to

Abraham's country and select a bride from his own kith and kin. The minister of the gospel who would find a bride for Christ cannot find her in the world, but he must seek her among the people of God. The children of God may be found in the world and called out of the world to repentance; but the bride of Christ must be found among God's people.

It is the highest duty and privilege of God's ministry to lead the children of the kingdom up out of childhood into bridehood. The Church is the bride of Christ; she must be separated from the world; she must exalt Jesus Lord of all. To be a prolific bride, to become a travailing Zion, bringing forth children born of the Spirit and nursing them up into man and womanhood in Christ, she must be fully consecrated, and wholly sanctified. Christ must be her Ishi indeed.

The Bible frequently uses human connections in order to convey to our minds the sacred relationship that may exist between God and His people. In the parable of the prodigal son the relationship of father and son is used to show how the heart of God yearns for those who have gone astray, and how, with open arms, he receives the returning penitent. The relation of husband and wife, one of the most sacred that can possibly exist between human beings, is taken by the Apostle Paul to instruct us in the profound mystery of Christ's union with love for and protection over His Church. Listen to the inspired apostle: "Husbands, love your wives, even as Christ also loved the church, and gave himself for it: that he might sanctify and cleanse it with the washing of water by the word, that he might present it to himself a glorious church, not having spot, or wrinkle, or any such thing; but that it should be holy and without blemish."

We can conceive of no illustration more illuminating or language more clear and forceful than is here used by the holy Apostle to teach us the intimate and sacred relationship that should exist between Christ and His Church. The minister of the gospel is under sacred oath and a solemn obligation to labor

with all the power that God may give him
to bring the Church of Christ up into this
spiritual realm of purity, devotion, and
loyal love to her Master and Bridegroom.

Can one conceive of greater treachery
than that Eliezer, the servant of Abraham, should have turned aside from his
sacred mission, and in spite of his oath
to Abraham, had sought out some
Canaanitish family and proposed for
financial, or other selfish advantages, to
take some impure and unconsecrated
woman, thus deceiving his master, bring
back to Isaac a Canaanitish heathen for
his bride. Eliezer had no such thought;
the whisper of such temptation would
have filled him with horror. But he
would not have been more false to the
solemn oath he had taken, or more deceptive in his treatment of his young
master, if he had have practiced such
deception, than would be the minister of
the gospel if he gathered into the Church,
by all sorts of schemes and inducements
for his own advantage, an impenitent and
unregenerated people, and tried to foist
them upon the Lord, as if they were His

true bride, when in fact, they are strangers and aliens.

The office of the ministry is most honorable. There can be no higher calling; but it is a sacred and solemn office. It is one in which a man enters into a covenant with the God who called him, which he dare not break or trifle with. He bears the message of the Lord; the jewelry which he carries comes. from the storehouse of divine truth. He is on a sacred mission of highest and holiest character. He is led of the Holy Spirit in a search for a bride for Christ. He must go, breathing an earnest prayer for guidance. He must use the greatest wisdom and care. He must make haste; invitations to tarry and to feast must not detain him from pressing on the pathway of duty. He must be filled with an insatiate desire for the perfecting of the saints. He must know something of what the Apostle Paul expresses in Gal. 4:19, when he says, "My little children, of whom I travail in birth again until Christ be formed in you." The Apostle was in a holy agony of love and solicitude that these children born of the Spirit through his gospel message, should be established in the faith and Christ should be "formed in them."

God wants a holy Church; a Church separated from the world; a Church which has taken the vow of glad and happy union with His Son, and which has kept, and is keeping, those vows inviolate. Such a Church will be fruitful. She will have periods of holy longing and earnest prayer for revivals of religion; she cannot be content without seeing children born into the kingdom. She will love and nurse them into spiritual strength and development. She will bring up her children into bridehood with the Master. She will scorn the attractions and enticements of all who would woo her away from her betrothed. She is contented only with His blessing; she is happy in His service. She arrays herself for His pleasure; she seeks His glory and rejoices in His love.

Such a Church will be filled with power. The world will recognize her as the bride of Christ. She will indeed be the salt of the earth and the light of the world, and men seeing her good works, will glorify God. She will move in majesty through the earth, saving the lost, healing the sick, feeding the hungry, clothing the naked, visiting the imprisoned, homing the orphan, rebuking sin, lifting up the fallen, rescuing the perishing, fulfilling the great purpose of God in giving His Son to redeem the Church and sanctify it unto Himself, "Fair as the moon, clear as the sun, and terrible as an army with banners."

The thought of Eliezer seeking to put himself in Isaac's place, to woo the heart of Rebekah away from his master, and seduce her from her holy love and devotion to Isaac, is almost too repulsive to entertain, and yet, this thought has its place in discussing this all-important subject. There is the possibility of a minister forgetting the supremacy of the Master, of the spirit of selfishness creeping into the heart of the man who ought to exalt his Lord, high over all; and the very man who should lead the Church into holy bridehood, seducing the Church so as that she will gratify his own carnal lusts for pelf and play.   We grant you, that the thought is revolting, but nevertheless it must be pressed upon our minds.

Think of a minister of the gospel becoming so blind to the duties of his holy office, so neglectful of his solemn vows, that instead of striving to lead the Church into the consecration and holy purity of the bride of Christ, he should seek to comfort her in her negligence; he should teach her that entire consecration to her Lord is not to be expected; that holiness, through the agonies of His love on the cross, is impossible; that she cannot be entirely separated from the sinful customs and habits of the world about her; that she is to follow the fashions and seek the pleasures of the world which crucified her Lord.

Startling as is the thought, it must be admitted that in not a few churches this very thing has happened, and many congregations have been led away from the Christ by false teachers. They have not been renewed and kept up in membership by the holy travails of a sanctified Zion, bringing God's spiritual children into His kingdom, but these congregations have been kept up by many schemes of inducing sinners and worldlians to unite with the Church, who know nothing of spiritual birth and the renewings of the Holy Ghost. To use the strong language of the apostle, such persons are "Bastards and not sons." What could be more fearful than that a man called of God to seek a bride for Christ, that she may be presented in her holy virginity without spot or wrinkle, should become the seducer of the bride and should lead her away by false teachings and practices into disloyalty and divorcement from her holy bridehood. How fearful for such a man to appear in the presence of his Master in that awful day of accounts, when all facts shall be published, and all secrets revealed, and he stands condemned before the court of heaven because he has not labored, prayed, and ministered "To the end that he may establish your hearts unblameable in holiness before God, even our Father, at the coming of our Lord Jesus Christ with all his saints."

We can but believe that there are not a few ministers of our day who are entertaining the Church rather than teaching her; who are amusing their people rather than warning them; who are comforting them in their sins rather than calling them unto holiness; who are making their church houses places of play and pastime instead of places of repentance and worship; who are busy with many things and entirely neglecting the *one* thing that, "holiness without which no man shall see the Lord;" that consecration of life and purity of heart, without which the Church cannot be the fruitful and nursing mother of the children of the true kingdom.

Some years ago, there came to a certain southern city an enterprising man from an Eastern state. He bought a large interest in a factory and was made overseer of an important department. He found a temporary home in a large boarding house run successfully by an enterprising woman, who had hired at small wages, for her cook an orphan and dependent sister. The orphan girl was a graceful and beautiful creature, but the elder sister who owned and controlled the establishment, was given to driving and scolding. Her numerous children were constantly annoying their young auntie, and crying to their mother to "make auntie do this and that." The gentleman from the East took note of these things; at first his indignation was aroused for the rosy-cheek cook. Later, it warmed into a tender sympathy, and later still, it bloomed out into a devoted love. From time to time, he sought opportunity for conversation. He found the orphan girl serving in the kitchen, not only of great beauty but with unusual mental gifts and many fascinating attractions. In due time courtship followed; his love was reciprocated and an engagement of marriage was made. A beautiful gold ring was placed upon the customary engagement finger. This was a *consecration* ring. It was a witness to the girl of her betrothal, of the fact that she belonged to the man who had won her heart. It was a witness to her lover that her affections were settled and fixed; it was a witness to all other lovers to cease their attentions and wooings.

As the spring opened the lover said to the beautiful orphan girl, "You shall not slave in this hot kitchen during the summer. We must be married." The girl objected and postponed the time of their wedding until early winter, hoping by that time to save out of her meager earnings sufficient to purchase her bridal robes. But the lover, a man of large means, insisted upon an early wedding, and finally the date was fixed. Just three weeks from the Thursday evening he took train to visit his mother, with the promise that three weeks hence "I will return at eight o'clock in the evening to claim you for my bride."

Just before leaving the lover tossed a bundle upon the centertable and said: "There's a keepsake for you during my absence." Forgetting the bundle, the beautiful orphan climbed the steps to her little sleeping apartment under the rafters, opened a secret drawer and counted the handful of nickels, dimes and quarters which she had accumulated. She then said to herself, "Three weeks from this evening I am to become the bride of this handsome and wealthy gentleman. His friends will be present. I have no means to equip myself fittingly for the occasion. My costume will embarrass my husband." Having no one to whom she might turn for assistance, she broke into tears. Remembering the package he had thrown on the table, she hastened down the stairway, caught up the keepsake, and returned hurriedly to her room, and with locked door, she opened the package, when to her surprise, there poured out a great heap of twenty dollar gold pieces. As she looked upon the glittering wealth, she exclaimed, "Knowing that I am but a poor orphan girl he has not only given me the wedding ring, but he has also provided for me the wedding robe."

She at once put the dressmakers to work. During the weeks of his absence there were no flirtations with other suitors, but the time was occupied with joyous preparation for her lover's return to claim her as his happy bride. Her sister and the family ridiculed her and said, "This Yankee will never return. Why should he wish to marry you? He is one of the handsomest men in the city, and he is rich. Why should he seek for his bride a poor orphan girl, a cook in a boarding house kitchen?" "Yes," said the betrothed girl, "He is handsome and he is wealthy, but he loves me and I have the witness that he will come again and take me to himself."

The appointed evening came and the bride arrayed herself in the beautiful and spotless robe her lover had provided; and while her sister and other members of the family were ridiculing her because of her preparation and her joyful anticipation, and assuring her that her promised bridegroom would never come, the carriages, bearing him and his friends rolled about the doors of the boarding house. The bridegroom ran up the steps, the minister and his friends attending him, and the marriage ceremony was performed amidst the confusion, tears and sobs of the surprised and startled family; and before they could realize what had occurred the orphan girl, their beautiful cook, hectored and driven at a pitiful wage, was caught away and had become the wife of a wealthy gentleman, the mistress of a splendid home.

This incident in a family well known to this preacher, illustrates the situation of the true Church of the Lord Jesus Christ, which is not a denomination of professed followers of our Lord, but is the real bride of Christ made up of all true believers of all denominations and creeds, who have known the regenerating grace and sanctifying power of the Holy Ghost; who are separate from the world and clothed in the linen, pure and white, which is the righteousness of the saints. The thought of the bridehood of the Church was in the mind of Isaiah when he said, "Fear not; for thou shalt not be ashamed: neither be thou confounded; for thou shalt not be put to shame: for thou shalt forget the shame of thy youth, and shalt not remember the reproach of thy widowhood any more. For thy Maker

is thine husband; and the Lord of hosts is his name; and thy Redeemer the Holy One of Israel; the God of the whole earth shall he be called. For the Lord hath called thee as a woman forsaken and grieved in spirit, and a wife of youth, when thou wast refused, saith thy God."
—Isa. 54:4-6.

The prophet is here comforting Israel, but Israel represents the Church, the bride of Christ. The Apostle Paul expresses the feeling that should possess the heart of every minister who, faithful to the covenant vows of his holy office, is seeking to bring the Church up into holy union with the Lord Jesus. The Apostle's language is beautiful and loaded with deepest meaning when he says, "For I am jealous over you with a godly jealousy: for I have espoused you unto one husband, that I may present you as a chaste virgin to Christ."

This must be the attitude of the true Church, "a chaste virgin" espoused to her Lord, separated from the world, arrayed in white, living in expectation, rejoicing in hope, and ready to meet her Lord as

He comes in His triumph with shouts of praise.

Pity on the man called to the holy ministry who would seduce the bride of his Lord, persuade her that she need not expect His coming, defile her with sin, fill her thought and desire with worldly ambitions and pursuits, until he betroth her to mammon and blot out of her heart the desire and "blessed hope" of the return of her Bridegroom.

GOD'S PLAN FOR A REVIVAL

"And Samuel spake unto all the house of Israel, saying, If ye do return to the Lord with all your hearts, then put away the strange gods and Ashtaroth from among you, and prepare your hearts unto the Lord, and serve him only: and he will deliver you out of the hand of the Philistines."—1 Sam. 7:3.

We must have a revival or a revolution. We have not at the present time enough true spiritual salt to permeate and save this nation. There must be a great spiritual awakening or, the decay of morals, the increase of selfishness, and finally, a tremendous social upheaval. The sea of human life is seething with counter current; the billows of prejudice and passion are rolling high. The conflict between capital and labor, the skeptical teaching in seats of learning, the uncertain sound in pulpits, the worldliness crowding into the churches, the immodesty and lewdness thrusting itself upon society, the widespread looseness of family government, the recklessness in the expenditure of money and pleasure seeking among the rising generation, the boldness of the criminal classes, the mob spirit breaking out in all parts of the nation, with all the counter currents of dissatisfaction and unrest among the masses of the people, have produced a tempest in this nation that can only be calmed and put at rest by the authoritative voice of the divine Master. Hence, the statement in the beginning of this discourse—we must have a revival or we shall have a revolution. There must be a widespread and deep spiritual awakening in this nation, calling men back to faith in the Bible as the word of God, and obedience to that word, and trust in Jesus Christ for salvation, the cultivation and practice of His teachings under the leadership and empowering of the Holy Spirit in every-day life, or growing worse, our nation on a moral downgrade, will plunge into some tremendous catastrophe of ruin.

The feeling is widespread among thoughtful people everywhere, that nothing short of a great revival of Bible religion can meet the emergencies of the hour. This is not only true with reference to religious teachers, but business men in the wider realms of commercialism and large vision in material matters, are beginning to realize that in order to preserve the foundations of society, maintain commercial integrity and keep order among the masses of humanity, there must be a turning back to faith and obedience to the teaching of the Ten Commandments and the Sermon on the Mount. Hence, intelligent selfishness is pleading for a religious awakening that will insure national progress and the safety of investments and business enterprises.

Men are awakening to the fact that to forget God is to invite ruin; that "Righteousness exalteth a nation, but sin is a reproach to any people." They are coming to appreciate the exhortation of King David to Israel when he stood up and delivered to them his last great address: "Now therefore in the sight of all Israel the congregation of the Lord, and in the audience of our God, keep and seek for all the commandments of the Lord your God: that ye may possess this good land, and leave it for an inheritance for your children after you forever."—1 Chron. 28:8.

The multitudes are not thinking of God, of the danger of sin and the wickedness of it.   The multitudes are seeking after money and pleasure.   They are kindling to brighter burning the maddening flames of covetous and lustful desires for the temporal things that perish.   They have forgotten God, but serious men and women, everywhere, in all walks and classes of life, are coming to a union of opinion and oneness of conclusion that the only possible remedy for existing conditions is a deep, widespread revival of Bible religion.

Many preachers have undertaken to fill the empty pews of their churches by installing moving pictures.   The crowds have come to attend the shows but have not remained to pray.   In many places they have turned churches into social centers; there have been feasts and carousals but there was not salt to save and sanctify the gay and thoughtless throngs who desecrated the temples of the Lord by making them houses of carnival and amusement.   Many things have been suggested as remedies for the untoward situation; it has even been proposed that we have a widespread revival of religion, "Without tears and with no shouting at all."   Many people have been brought into the church by one means and another, persuasions, decisions, and professions without the deep conviction wrought in the sinner's soul by the truth of God and the regenerating power of the Holy Ghost.   There can be no method that will lead more certainly to the final paralysis of the church, the undermining and destroying of Christianity, than the bringing of unregenerated masses of people into the church.

If we are to have a revival that will save the people, permeate the whole moral atmosphere, sanctify the home, introduce the spirit of integrity and hon-

esty into commerce, produce civic righteousness and elevate the ideals of the
people, and make firm the foundations of
our great republic, such a revival must
regenerate the hearts of men; it must
bring men out of the kingdom of darkness into the kingdom of light; it must
change the heart of the individual; men
must seek and find the regenerating power
of the Holy Ghost; they must become in
Christ new creatures.

Such a revival as is here indicated is
quite possible. There are those who try
to convince us that times have changed,
that we are living in a new era of history;
that men must be approached from a different angle, that education can take the
place of regeneration, that culture and
human refinement must be substituted
for the sanctifying power of Jesus' blood.
All of this is shallow cant; every word of
it in contradiction of divine truth and
the great facts in human experience. God
never changes. He is the same yesterday,
today, and forever. Human nature is the
same. Customs may change, discoveries
in the field of science may be made, but

these things do not affect the heart; the natural heart of man remains desperately wicked. Jesus Christ stands in the midst of the age and declares, "Except ye be born again ye cannot see the kingdom of God."

If we have entered upon a new era of history we have brought over into it all the sins of the past era intensified. There never was more crime in the nation than at the present time. Sabbath desecration is fearfully on the increase; immodesty of dress on the streets, in the house of God, and in all public places is such an outrage against decency that the editors of secular papers are expressing surprise and disapproval; woman's clubs are registering their protest; devout ministers are lifting up their voices in rebuke; cartoonists are using their stencils in ridicule, and people are asking, when shall we reach the limit in the immodest apparel of our American womanhood? There is a dance craze throughout the nation, and the lewd embrace and improper contact of the sex in the dance halls and hotel ballrooms are of the most appalling and shocking character. The theater and moving picture are absolutely reeking with licentiousness and sowing broadcast among the multitudes of young people who crowd them, the seed that can but bring forth a harvest of unchastity that will head up in divorces, broken homes, wrecked families and blasted lives. If we are living in a new age, there has been brought over into it all the sinfulness and wickedness of the old age, intensified and quickened with a tenacity and aggressive boldness unknown before in the history of the American people. The obstacles which stand in the way of revivals of religion are not a new era, a change in God, or His methods of dealing with men; a change in human nature, or the needs of the soul of man; but the difficulty is in the perverseness of man and his effort to substitute notions and plans of his own in the place of the will and word of God.

Isaiah expresses the difficulty very clearly when he says, "Behold the Lord's hand is not shortened, that it cannot save; neither his ear heavy, that it cannot hear:

But your iniquities have separated between you and your God, and your sins have hid his face from you, that he will not hear. For your hands are defiled with blood, and your fingers with iniquity: your lips have spoken lies, your tongues have muttered perverseness."

If we are to save this nation from revolution, if we are to preserve the church from woful backsliding and salt modern society with the teachings and spirit of the religion of Jesus Christ, if we are to preserve the integrity of the home, maintain parental government, train the rising generation to obedience, the fear of God and righteous living; in a word, if this great nation is to abide in its integrity and continue to march at the head of the column of the progress of the world, and send forth spiritual life and blessing to heathen lands, we must have a great spiritual awakening, a genuine religious revival, and we had just as well turn *now* to the Bible, turn away from all human inventions and substitutes and find in the word of God the true pattern and safe direction for the means to be used to

secure the end so greatly needed and so
much desired.

Our text offers a solution to the whole
problem. It gives us a key that will un-
lock the situation and lead out into the
highway over which we may march to
certain and glorious victory. Following
the word of God we cannot fail.   David
strikes the keynote in the 81st Psalm
when he says, "But my people would not
hearken to my voice; and Israel would
none of me. So I gave them up to their
own hearts' lusts: and they walked in
their own counsels. O, that my people
had hearkened unto me, and Israel had
walked in my ways! I should soon have
subdued their enemies, and turned my
hand against their adversaries. The
haters of the Lord should have submitted
themselves unto him."

We see here that the obedience of God's
people would have brought the haters of
the Lord to submission and obedience to
Him. A holy church walking in harmony with the divine will and commandments, filled with the Spirit-breathing
love of Christ, will bring about spiritual

awakening and outpourings of power
which will subdue the wicked, bring them
to repentance and obedience before God.
But let us come closer to this text and note
carefully God's plan for a revival and the
gracious results when that plan is carried
out.

Israel had sinned; sin had brought
separation from God, and separation
from God had brought calamities thick
and fast. The armies of Israel were being defeated; the Ark of the Lord had
been captured. Eli, the backslidden and
easy-going priest, under whose lax guidance Israel had drifted into sin, had heard
the rebuke of the Lord and had fallen
dead when he heard of the capture of the
Ark. The Philistines had found the Ark
a curse to them; the Ark was of no avail
to any people who did not worship the
God of the Ark and keep the covenant
which was contained therein. The mere
emblems of our religion are worth nothing, if we cease to worship God in spirit
and in truth. The altars of the church
may become a curse if we desecrate those
altars with broken vows, and the very

house of God may become a snare if we transform it into a place of amusement, shows, pastimes, and the cultivation of sinful lusts instead of a place to learn the duties of the Christian life, to worship and to pray.

For twenty years the Ark of the Lord had been absent from the central place of worship. It had been kept in Kirjath-jearim, but now there appeared some very hopeful indications. The inspired record says, "All the house of Israel lamented after the Lord." This was indeed encouraging. When men begin to long after God their sins which separate them from Him become hateful. Samuel, noting this spirit of longing among the people, seized the opportunity to break in upon them with the text. Let us repeat it here: "And Samuel spake unto all the house of Israel, saying, if ye do return unto the Lord with all your hearts, then put away the strange gods and Ashtaroth from among you, and prepare your hearts unto the Lord, and serve him only: and he will deliver you out of the hand of the Philistines."

We find the direction of Samuel very clear and positive. The inspired writer tells us that the people obeyed; they put away their idols; they turned wholly to the Lord, and Samuel gathered Israel to Mizpeh and prayed to the Lord for them. The people fasted and prayed and said, "We have sinned against the Lord." The Philistines heard of the gathering and prayers of the Israelites and went up to destroy them; the people were in great distress and plead with Samuel, saying, "Cease not to cry unto the Lord our God for us, that he will save us out of the hand of the Philistines." Then Samuel offered a young lamb as a burnt-offering and continued his prayers for Israel. As Samuel was offering the lamb and pouring out his prayers, "The Philistines drew near to battle against Israel;" and "The Lord thundered with a great thunder on that day upon the Philistines, and discomfitted them; and they were smitten before Israel. Then the Israelites pursued them and smote them, and Samuel set up an Ebenezer stone, saying, Hitherto hath the Lord helped us."

This was a genuine revival. Let us note the steps. First of all, the people "Lamented after the Lord." They realized their sinfulness; they longed for the restoration of the Ark, for communion and comfort. They applied to their religious teachers for help and guidance. Fortunately, Samuel was not a compromiser. It never occurred to him to suggest human inventions to take the place of the divine plan. God only was able to bring deliverance, restoration and blessing.

Samuel called upon the people to forsake their sins; to put away their strange gods. "They must prepare their hearts unto the Lord, and serve him only." There must be no half-way measures. All idols must be cast away and God must have absolute authority. The Israelites obeyed the commandment of Samuel, and then gave themselves to confession, repentance and prayer. At this juncture they met with great opposition. The Philistines became uneasy and set themselves to break in upon these revival processes. The backslidden people were in an agony of fear and plead for help from God.

Samuel took a young lamb and offered it in burnt-offering. There must be an atonement made for sin. Now, that the Israelites have "Lamented after him," obeyed the voice of His servant, "Put away their strange gods," confessed their sins, given themselves to fasting and prayer, and Samuel offers up the atoning lamb, God comes upon the scene. The Philistines have drawn near to battle; they little realize that they are about to have to contend with the Almighty. The artillery of heaven broke loose upon them; God thundered with a great thunder upon the Philistines. This was no ordinary thunder; it was the voice of the Almighty in crashing wrath against the enemies of His repentant and praying people.

The Philistines understood that this was not common thunder for a shower of rain, but that the Almighty was speaking to them in the boom of His indignation. They were filled with fear and fled for their lives. God can speak to men so that they recognize His voice. There is an inner ear to the human soul that can detect the tone of the supernatural, that quakes and quails before the voice of the Almighty. No man, or army of men, can march up against the artillery of the skies when God thunders in His indignation against their sins and in the defense of His people.

Here we have the scriptural plan of a revival. The church should lament after God, long for Him, desire to feel the power and glory of His presence. She should listen with attentive ear to the voice of His ministry, and, O, how important that that ministry be faithful. She should be obedient and purge herself from sin. She needs to fast, confess, and pray and remember the atonement made by the Lamb of God in the agonies of Calvary, and then she may expect God to come upon the scene in His supernatural power.

We ought not to expect a widespread revival from the Lord while we keep in our college and university chairs men who deny the inspiration of the Scriptures and who destroy the faith of the students who are under them for instruction. If Protestantism of these United States wants a mighty spiritual awakening and a great blessing from God, let her have the honesty, the candor and the courage to remove all destructive critics from her theological seminaries. Let her speak with no uncertain sound to those ministers who make light of her fundamental doctrines, and those new theology men who are introducing all sorts of human philosophies and dangerous heresies among the people. Let her purge her universities, her theological seminaries and her pulpits of the priests of Balaam, of her idol worshippers. Let her have a holy courage and zeal for God that will not hesitate to cut off her right hand and pluck out her right eye, if need be. Let her reverence and respect true piety, rather than wealth, and loyalty to the Bible, rather than those smart fellows who are discounting Moses, St. Paul, and worse still, the teaching and authority of the Lord Jesus Christ.

If Protestantism wants a revival let her

ministry preach mightily against the wickedness of our times. Let them in holy fearlessness denounce the immodest dress, the lewd dance, the impure theater, the vices of the card table, the wicked lusts and high tide of worldliness on every hand. If she would have God come upon her with a great spiritual awakening, let them pitch their moving picture machines into a dump heap, tear the theatrical platforms from the sanctuary of the Lord, clear out their basketball teams from God's house, and give herself to repentance, to fasting, and to prayer.

Let us be done with all the shallow talk about new methods and unscriptural substitutes for the religion of the Lord Jesus. Let us say less about *decisions* and more about repentance. Let us say less about *confessions* of Christ and more about pardoning mercy and regenerating grace. Let our ministry have a holy courage to warn the people in harmony with the plain teaching of our Lord Jesus, that those who live and die in their sins will wake up in the fires of eternal torment. However, the Philistines may

come against us, let us be true to God
and His word, rally around the cross in
prayer until God comes upon the scene
with the thunder of His power. God can
rebuke the destructive critics, the false
teachers, the movie mongers, the church
theatricals, the gaudy, godless gang in
their pageants and plays. They can no
more stand the thunderings of the Almighty than the heathen Philistines. We
need a revival beginning in deep longings
after God, followed up with repentance,
confession, fasting and prayer, and
climaxed by the manifestation of the
divine presence, by the thunder of God's
indignation against sin, by the glorious
manifestation of the Holy Ghost in the
salvation of the people.

Nothing can meet the emergency of the
times except such revival as is here indicated. Any sort of human schemes and
enticements to bring impenitent and unregenerated people into the church is only
to burden the church with hindering
weights and sink her deeper into backsliding and worldliness. We must have
a revival or we shall have a revolution.

The great multitudes of discontented and restless people of this nation must be salted with the pure gospel of Jesus, must be saved by the power of the Holy Spirit, or confusion will be worse confused, bitter prejudices will continue to increase; there will be class hatred, social upheaval, blood and fire.

When a people trample upon God's holy Word, reject His Son, refuse His mercy and grieve His Spirit away from them they become self-destructive; there is no need for the fearful judgments of the Lord to be visited upon them. The most fearful judgment that can fall upon a people is for God to withdraw Himself, to simply leave them alone, and they will rise in wrath against each other, pluck the keystone from the arch of civilization and let the whole social fabric come crashing down upon them.

Shall we have a revival? Will the ministry plead with the people and warn them? Can the church of America be brought to lament after the Lord? Will we come to fasting and prayer and confession of sins? Will we turn away from all subterfuges and sweep away the miserable substitutes for the gospel of Christ and the atonement of Christ? Shall we gather about His pierced feet in worship and faith and prayer until our God shall come into our midst in the glory of His power, rebuking the Philistines of sin, putting to rout the enemies of truth and righteousness? Then will He pour out His Spirit upon His Church, and bring by the regenerating power of the Holy Spirit, multitudes of sinners into the kingdom, sanctifying His people with the blood of Jesus, filling them with the Holy Ghost and making them nursing fathers and mothers in Israel to develop the newborn babes of the kingdom into men and women in Christ. Then, indeed, we could set up our Ebenezer stone and shouting around it could declare like Samuel of old, "Hitherto hath the Lord helped us."

NATIONAL SECURITY

"Now therefore in the sight of all Israel the congregation of the Lord, and in the audience of our God, keep and seek for all the commandments of the Lord your God: that ye may possess this good land, and leave it for an inheritance for your children after you forever."—First Chron. 28:8.

King David was approaching the close of a most remarkable career. He was delivering his last public address to his people; it was at the installation of Solomon as king of Israel. David stood up in the presence of the elders, the officers of his army, and the multitudes of the people, and spoke to them of the building of the temple, and exhorted them with reference to their conduct after his departure.

He reaches a climax in the Scripture which we have chosen for our text. In this verse he gives them to understand that their title to the land rests in their obedience to God; in order to keep the land, and hand it down to their posterity, they must "keep and seek for all of the commandments of the Lord their God." Without the divine favor they were not to hope to possess their goodly heritage, and they were not to expect the divine favor without obedience to the divine commandments.

They were to give diligence in this matter; they were with care and pains-taking to search the Word of God, to acquaint themselves with His law, and to keep all of His commandments. He assured them that this was a safe guarantee to their possessions and the entailment of their inheritance to their children after them forever.

All Bible readers are acquainted with the tragic and sad history of the Israelites. They became a backslidden people; they violated their covenant with God; they forgot His commandments and trampled upon His laws; directly, the kingdom was rent in twain; there was war, bloodshed, and strife, and by and by, their hillsides were covered with the tents of heathen invaders, and their valleys trembled under the charge of the chariots of their victorious enemies, who conquered and desolated Israel. Carried into captivity, they were sold in the various Gentile countries until the slave markets were glutted with captive Hebrews.

It is said that upon one occasion old King William, the grandfather of the dethroned Kaiser, during one of his campaigns, while sitting at his campfire at night, said to his chaplain, "Chaplain, give me, in a word, the best external evidence of the inspiration of the Scriptures. I am not asking for a discussion or an argument, but give me in a condensed statement the strongest external evidence that the Bible is an inspired book." It is said that the chaplain saluted and said, "Sire, the Jews!" "Ha!" said the old emperor, "That is excellent. You could not have answered better. The Jews, as we have them in Bible, in prophecy, in profane history and modern times, are one of the most powerful proofs that the Bible is inspired."

The chaplain's answer was good, and the Emperor's comment was correct. The history of the Jews from the prophecies of Moses, as he led them from Egyptian bondage and foretold, even before they entered into Canaan of their backslidings, their captivity, and dispersion, have been through the centuries a living witness to the divine inspiration of their holy prophets who pointed out the calamities that would befall them because of their disobedience to the commandments of God.

The history of the Hebrew people stands out as a monument of the fact that sin will bring ruin to a people; that however God may love a nation and bestow His divine favors upon it, that when it violates His commandments and tramples upon His laws, He can but punish it; that His divine favor must be secured and kept by obedience to His commandments. God never created a greater people than the Jews, and He never will. They were a chosen people; they were greatly favored; through them God proposed to reveal Himself to the world. They reached a climax of greatness during the reign of Solomon. People from afar, learning of the wisdom of Solomon, the splendor and glory of his reign, came and listened to his wise sayings, looked upon the magnificence of the temple and the splendor of his palace, to return and carry the intelligence of his greatness, and the supremacy and glory of the God he worshipped to the ends of the earth.

Had the Jews remained true and obedient to their God, the influence they would have wielded throughout the East, and their power to have affected for good the heathen nations about them, would be interesting, indeed, to contemplate; but backsliding and falling into sin, they became the easy victims of the people they should have blessed, and their desolated lands, scattered and persecuted people, have stood through the centuries as a witness to all nations that those who trample upon the divine commandments must expect to suffer the divine judgments.

We feel impressed that the text is especially applicable to this great nation of ours, and at this time. It seems imperative that the attention of the American people should be called to the fact that if we would possess this goodly heritage and leave to our children after us, we must "Seek and keep all the commandments of the Lord our God."

I well remember that when a small boy, my grandfather whose grandfather fell at the battle of Brandywine, fighting for the freedom of the American colonies, and who was a great patriot, said to me, "My son, there is no nation that can measure arms with this great republic. America can whip the world. If all the nations in civilization should combine and undertake to invade these shores, our brave people could meet and beat them all. We are unconquerable." I looked at my grandfather with admiration and my boy heart was thrilled with delight; my bosom swelled with pride at the thought of the greatness of my nation and its all-sufficient power to protect and defend itself.

Possibly my grandfather was mistaken. It may be that, as a boy, I was deluded, but I have not been fully able to recover from that delusion, if it be such. To speak plainly, I have no fear of any foreign foe invading successfully the sacred soil of our great republic; but I do fear that we have in the incubator of our social conditions the eggs that will hatch the serpents that might sting us to death. "If God be for us who can be against us?" The history of Israel stands there as a witness that we cannot hope to have the benediction and protection of God if we are not obedient to His commands. And the man must be blind, indeed, who does not see that sin is rampant throughout our beloved country.

God has spoken plainly with reference to the observation of the Sabbath. "Remember the Sabbath day, to keep it holy." We are becoming a nation of Sabbath breakers. If there were no violation of the Sabbath except the matter of public travel upon the trains, that itself would be a fearful violation of the third commandment. It is folly to argue that civilization has reached a stage of progress so that it has become necessary to violate the Sabbath day. Civilization must not undertake to dictate to God, or to rescind or revise the laws He has written for our government. It has been demonstrated that this law of the Sabbath is not only written in the Bible, but it is written in the physical nature of man. God who built man and understands his needs knew that he would need rest, and He appointed a day of rest. The man who ignores this law must suffer the consequences, not only in his soul but in his body. God also takes into consideration the welfare of those animals He has so graciously created to serve man, and He has commanded us that the beasts of burden shall have a day of rest. This law is specific for maid-servants, man-servants and beasts.

Our great railroad systems utterly ignore this commandment; they do not remember the Sabbath, to keep it holy, and millions of our people make the Sabbath day a day for travel on business and pleasure bent. The stations along the railway systems are crowded with boisterous throngs of people who have forgotten God, who care nothing for the third commandment, and, we regret to say, that many ministers of the gospel seem to have no conscience whatever on this subject. Since the automobile has come into use tens of thousands of church members absent themselves from the holy sanctuary and spend the Lord's day joy-riding, sight-seeing and picnicing. Throughout the baseball season countless throngs of people gather at the baseball parks on the Sabbath in our great cities and country towns for this exciting sport, shout and yell like mad heathens entirely oblivious of God and His day, and His commandment to keep the Sabbath holy.

The American people are rapidly becoming more indifferent on this subject. Stores and marts of trade are kept open; the hammer and saw are heard in the erection of buildings; theaters are crowded, the moving picture show does its largest business and dance halls are thronged with noisy crowds of thoughtless sinners who have forgotten there is a God, and who are indifferent to His commandments.

Can we suppose for a moment that the

God of this universe, the omnipotent and infinite Being who has written His law, not to lay a yoke upon us, but for our upbuilding and blessing, will be indifferent with reference to the desecration of the Sabbath? It is unthinkable that He should be. His delayed judgments do not indicate for a moment that He is indifferent or will forget to visit those who trample upon His commandments. "The Lord is merciful and gracious, slow to anger, and plenteous in mercy. He will not always chide: neither will he keep his anger for ever." He bears with men, He warns them, but by and by, He lays the axe to the root of the tree.

The taking of God's name in vain is positively forbidden. God has said He will not hold those guiltless who profane His name. This nation reeks with profanity from one end to the other. Those of us who travel up and down the land are startled at the reckless way in which men profane the holy name of our Creator. Small boys may be heard swearing on every hand, and it has come to pass in recent years, that many women are shockingly profane. The fiction of the times, and articles in leading magazines abound in horrible profanity. Men in their conceits have come to believe that it adds tone and zest to their writings to put most blasphemous expressions into the mouths of their fictitious characters. The judgments of God are bound to be visited upon a profane people. No self-respecting God can write down His laws and attach to them penalties, and suffer those laws to be constantly and flagrantly violated, and fail to inflict the penalties attached to them.

No devout and serious man can view with indifference and complacency the manner in which marriage vows are disregarded throughout this nation. The divorce court mill grinds constantly. Let any one for one week read the news items on the one subject of divorces, sought and granted, in any twenty of the large cities of this country, and he will be appalled; and divorces are by no means confined to our cities. In town, village and country place marriage ties are broken and tens of thousands of families are rent asunder; society reeks with the foul sin of adultery. One would think from reading the news of the divorce courts that God had nothing whatever to say on the subject of the sacredness of marriage. We do not like to introduce into this sermon any statements with reference to the vast numbers of young women who are being led astray. In this regard, things were bad enough before the war, but during and since the war illicit love, with all its sickening and disgusting seduction, blasting and ruining womanhood, has reached a high tide which is appalling, and cries to heaven for rebuke.

We doubt if there is a country beneath the sun, civilized or heathen, where children are more disobedient and less under the restraint and control of parents than in these United States. Children nowhere enjoy advantages equal to the children of this country; but a large per cent of them, male and female, in their early teens assume control of themselves, and walk roughshod over the laws, the entreaties and warnings of their parents.

The result is inevitable evil. God has spoken on this subject. Sinners of this character will bring down destruction upon their own heads.

"Thou shalt not steal" is a plainly written law, but it is said, and we fear is largely true, that we are becoming a nation of thieves. The profiteering during the world war revealed the startling state of greed and avarice among our great captains of industry. The vast millions of dollars filched from the people by the owners of the great coal mines during the winter of 1920 and 1921 staggers the imagination. Only think of the dishonesty in the sugar market during the years of 1919 and 1920. The public was robbed of hundreds of millions of dollars by the men who hoarded and controlled the sugar. It is said, and there is good reason to believe, that the dishonest evading of taxes is very common. Some time ago I was preaching in one of the great cities of this country and a young man who was clerking in a large department store came to me and said, that there were such misrepresentation of facts in the prices of goods in the "mark down" sales that he could not possibly discharge the duties of a salesman without constantly lying to the customers. In another city, where we tried to set up Bible standards of every-day conduct, a group of clerks remarked that "The preachers may be able to live honestly; but they could not come into the store where we clerk and practice what they preach and hold their position with our employers." There are, no doubt, honest merchants; we hope many of them, but dishonesty and trickery in trade are widespread and common about us everywhere. Multitudes of our fellow-beings are living in absolute disregard of God's positive commandment—"Thou shalt not steal."

Standing upon the lookout tower of the gospel ministry, seeking in the fear of God and the love of man to point out the evils which not only destroy the souls of our fellows, but menace the welfare and stability of our civil institutions, we cannot satisfy our conscience without an allusion to the daily press. Many of our great newspapers are under the control and direction of men who are utterly without the fear of God before their eyes. Not long since I spent some time in New York City, and on a number of occasions I bought copies of the great dailies, took them to my room and scanned the editorial pages, hoping to find some moral salt, some editorial in which the writer lifted up his voice against the flood of evil; some warning against immorality; some reminder that God has some rights in His universe; some word of restraint and caution against the folly and frivolities of the times.

I searched in vain. I found a number of flings at prohibition, of innuendoes and insinuations which were anything but uplifting. This is a serious matter; the great newspapers wield a powerful influence on the public mind, and many of them are under the direction of the liquor interests. They fought prohibition to the last ditch, and even after prohibition law had been written into our Constitution they are seeking to break down the law, to bring it into public contempt; their sympathies are with the violators of the law; they are educating and encouraging people in the making and selling of intoxicants. The violaters of the prohibition laws of the country are hungry, greedy, wolves of society; they are dangerous and bloody men. They become altogether lawless; they do not hesitate to murder, and they know they have back of them, and working for them, the tremendous influence of a large part of a godless press that is aiding and abetting in their crime in order to secure the polluted dollars of the liquor interests. The people ought to rise in their might and rebuke these godless publications that are sowing broadcast the seeds of lawlessness and crime. Their evil influence upon the rising generation can hardly be estimated; it pours like a great tributary into the rising tide of the Mississippi of human depravity and wickedness that must be rebuked and hindered or the judgments of God will come down upon our nation.

We have fallen upon times when in public life we have more politicians than we have patriots; when men in public life

are more influenced by political prejudices than they are by public welfare;
and it comes to pass that in our national
capital the two great political parties, instead of combining their influence to pass
laws to restrain greed and secure the
advantage of the vast multitudes of our
population, to protect our country from
the inflow of a dangerous mass of for-
eigners and secure for the people reason-
able rates of transportation, and a just
wage as a reward for their toil, they spend
their time trying to hinder and prevent
wise and helpful legislation by the party
in power, so that they can discredit the
administration and win victory over their
opposition at the next election. Thus the
interests of the people are tossed to and
fro between selfish politicians instead of
being administered and guided by wise,
unselfish, and God-fearing statesmen.

The evils we have mentioned in this
discourse are not imaginary; they actually
exist and it were folly to overlook or be
indifferent to the fact of their existence.
We do not claim by any means to have
covered the situation, or pointed out all

of the dangers; but what we have said is ample to justify what is to follow. We are well aware that there is a class of people in this country who boast of their optimism, and who are ready to cry out "Pessimist" if any moral physician undertakes to indicate with candor and truthfulness the various ailments or spiritual diseases that affect our national life. But we are convinced that the sober and thoughtful people who hear us will agree that our text and reflections are in order; that there is imminent and real danger that we bring down the judgments of God upon us. It would be useless to point out the untoward conditions we have mentioned, if we failed to also point out the remedy. The good physician not only gives a careful diagnosis of the condition of his patient and acquaints himself with the disease, but with skilful care he prescribes the remedy which will arrest the disease and eradicate the cause of the same.

A remedy for the evils of our times which threaten the sanctity of our homes, the spirituality of our church, and the stability of our nation, is to be found in the Word of God, and nowhere else. Mere reformations and legislation will not meet the case or heal the patient. "There is balm in Gilead;" there is a holy salt that can permeate society and purge out the moral diseases that corrupt and threaten the life of the people. It is the Word of God. That Word is a sword that, in the hands of faithful Samuels, can hew in pieces the Agags of avarice, lawlessness and lust that would blight and destroy our fair land. We must look to the pulpit and not merely to the wranglings of politicians and enactments in legislative bodies. Faithful men of God in the sacred desk must lift up their voices and proclaim the truths of the Bible with such earnestness, such holy courage, and such divine unction, that the people will be compelled to hear and give heed to their words of rebuke, warning and entreaty. The ministry of the gospel must bring the American people to realize that God has rights in His universe; that He must be recognized and revered; that His commandments must be sought out and kept;

that obedience to His laws is the highway of all progress and blessing that can be helpful and endurable to the building up of human civilization, and the securing of lasting good and happiness.

The remedy for the evils of our times is to be found in preaching. Not the preaching of Eddyism, that there is no sin, no devil, no future place of punishment; not the preaching of Russellism, that the sinful will have opportunities for repentance and rescue in some other world in a future state after death; not the preaching of Evolution, that our ancestors were apes, that there has been no fall of the race, that our redemption is not to come through a sudden new birth, but through untold myriads of ages of gradual development; not the preaching of the modern destructive critics, that Moses did not write the Pentateuch, that Job never did exist, that the book of Daniel is a dream, that Jesus Christ was not divine, that the writings of the Apostles are not inspired and divine authority. The preaching of these false doctrines and vain and unscriptural philosophies can only sink us deeper in unbelief, irreverence and wickedness, and hasten the judgments of God in the doom of the nation.

God has said, "My word shall not return unto me void." We need men in the pulpit who believe the Bible, who will unhesitatingly and fearlessly proclaim the word of the Lord. It is quick and powerful. It is the sword of the Spirit; its brilliant flash will dazzle the eye, and put to flight the armies of Sabbath breakers, blasphemers, adulterers, profiteers, and sinners. We need not fear what men can do if the pulpits of this nation will awake and cry mightily against the evils of our times. In a peculiar sense the men in the pulpit hold the destiny of the nation in their hands; if they prove recreant to their sacred and holy task then wickedness will increase, the tides of evil will rise higher, history will repeat itself, and our Ship of State will add another wreck to those that strew the rocky shores of time; but if the American pulpit will keep before the people, fixed in their minds and hearts, the great truths of our text, our homes will be pure and happy, our church will be the spiritual and consecrated bride of Christ, the foundations of our republic will remain secure, and our American civilization, with the banner of the Cross, and the Stars and Stripes, will march at the head of the column of world civilization and progress.

GOD'S SURE FOUNDATION

"If the foundations be destroyed, what can the righteous do?"—Psalm 11-3.

The foundation is that part of a building upon which the entire superstructure rests. The stability of the building depends upon the care and solidity with which the foundation is laid. If a man build a mere summer shack by a fishing stream in the woods for a few weeks' habitation, he gives little or no attention to foundation work. If he erects a cottage for permanent residence he must dig below the frost line and build up with well-placed and securely cemented stone. If his structure be larger he must go deeper and lay broader and more substantial foundation work. If he should undertake the erection of a modern steel-frame, concrete skyscraper he must go down into the depths and lay his foundation upon the solid rocks which hold the fabric of our earth intact in its flight through space.

100

When David wrote the 11th Psalm, the Church of God under the old dispensation had been making progress for a number of centuries. David was her chief poet and hymn writer. The foundations to which he refers were those revealed truths that God had given to seers and prophets from the days of Abraham to the times in which the Psalmist wrote. David was not only poet but prophet also. He not only looked backward to the revelation which God, from time to time, had given to His people, but he looked forward to the unfolding progress and development of the divine plan of redemption, tuned his harp and sang with joy of the coming Redeemer.

His songs reveal the fact that he was thoroughly acquainted with the past history of the Hebrews. He knew the story of Abraham's call and separation from his people; he declares that God "Made known his ways unto Moses, his acts unto the children of Israel." He points out that "Israel also came into Egypt, and Jacob sojourned in the land of Ham. And

he increased his people greatly; and made them stronger than their enemies. He turned their hearts to hate his people, to deal subtilly with his servants. He sent Moses his servant; and Aaron whom he had chosen. He showed his signs among them, and wonders in the land of Ham. He sent darkness, and made it dark; and they rebelled not against his word. He turned their waters into blood, and slew their fish. Their land brought forth frogs in abundance, in the chambers of their kings. He spake, and there came divers sorts of flies, and lice in all their coasts. He gave them hail for rain, and flaming fire in their land. He smote their vines also and their fig-trees; and brake the trees of their coasts. He spake, and the locusts came and caterpillars came, and that without number, and did eat up all the herbs in their land, and devoured the fruit of their ground. He smote all the first born of their land, the chief of all their strength. He brought them forth also with silver and gold; and there was not one feeble person among their tribe."
—105 Psa.

We have quoted at length from this Psalm and might go much farther to show that David, living fourteen generations after Abraham, was thoroughly acquainted with the history of his people, and God's revelations to them; and he claims these revelations of divine truth as the foundation upon which the whole superstructure of the Church of his time, and the promise and hope for the future, rests with absolute security. David was not a destructive critic. He accepted the writings of the Old Testament Scriptures which then existed as a reliable and trustworthy revelation from God. There were possibly doubters in his day, and those who would have discounted the history of the Hebrews, the revelations and law which God had given them through holy men of old, "who spake as they were moved by the Holy Ghost"

In our text David asks a pertinent and important question: "If the foundations be destroyed, what can the righteous do?" This is an important question today. The enemies of God and the Bible are assailing the Scriptures from every possible standpoint. They are writing question marks upon every page of divine revelation, both in Old Testament and New. Some one claiming to be a scholar with adequate equipment and thorough investigation has arisen to deny the call of Abraham, the inspiration of Moses, the divine origin of the Ten Commandments, the Deity of the Lord Jesus, the trustworthiness of the gospel, the authority of the epistles, the visitation to John the beloved on the Isle of Patmos, and the glorious truths contained in the Book of Revelation. There is no question but the infidels of our times are "Blasting at the Rock of Ages"

Whatever disagreements and contentions may exist among the disciples of Charles Darwin, whatever of unbelief and uncertainty may cloud the minds of the devotees of "Modern thought", however conflicting may be the views and philosophies of the apostles of the *New Theology*, one thing is absolutely certain—the writers of the Bible, Old Testament and New, believed in God and each other; and their teachings form a combination of unbreakable links in a golden chain of inspired truth stretching across the centuries from the fall of Adam in the Garden of Eden to the crucifixion of Jesus Christ upon the hill of Calvary; and from His resurrection at Joseph's new tomb to His coming in the clouds of glory.

The Church of the living God is "Built upon the foundation of the apostles and prophets, Jesus Christ himself being the chief cornerstone; in whom all the building fitly framed together groweth unto an holy temple in the Lord. In whom ye also are builded together for an habitation of God through the Spirit."—Eph. 2:20, 21, 22. The foundations of our faith are secure, and we have nothing to fear so long as we rest that faith upon the foundation of prophet, apostle, and Christ; but when we turn from the foundation truths of the Bible to chase after the will o' the wisp of modern philosophy we must sooner or later be lost in the bogs of unbelief and infidelity.

The enemies of God's truth would break the army of inspiration into separate divisions and make their attack in

detail.   The old infidelity was blasphemous; it sat in the back room of bar-
rooms, drank its liquor, blasphemed God,
ridiculed the Bible, and denied the Deity
of Jesus and the atonement He made for
sinful men upon the cross.   As the race
became more enlightened infidelity was
compelled to change its tactics; now it
sits in the chairs of universities and theological schools.   It often wears a clergy-
man's coat.   It plays the role of scholar-
ship and claims to be actuated by the love
of truth and the spirit of altruism.   It has
much to say of a "new era", of the necessity of giving up old doctrines and effete
notions in order to meet the exigencies
of a progressive age.   It has but little to
say of Sinai, of Calvary, and of coming
judgment.   It prates much about social
uplift and progress.   It is eager to amuse
and entertain the people; it proposes,
with its shows in the church, to empty the
theaters, and with its social dances and
merriments, to rob the dance hall and
elevate the pleasures of the world into
means of grace.

This "Modernism"—the apostles of

the new theology—boast that they "Do not believe in a 'slaughter-house religion' " By which they slur the sacred and solemn ceremonies of the Hebrew Church that emphasized that great truth, "Without the shedding of blood there is no remission of sins." These preachers of *negations* have little or nothing to say of the fall of man and the sinfulness of the human heart. They would teach us that man has ever fallen *upward*, and that his unholy uprisings are not the "remains of sin," but the outcroppings of the remains of the animal ancestry from which he came. Ignoring the Bible account of man's origin, they would have us believe that instead of coming forth from the plastic hand of God in the image of his Creator, that through some hundreds of millions of years he has gradually evolved from a bit of slime on the bottom of the deep; and instead of pointing him to Jesus Christ for the cleansing power of His sanctifying blood, they would bid him be patient to plod slowly on his upward way for countless ages toward a final perfection. These men say almost

nothing of sin and guilt, of repentance
and the new birth, of consecration, the
baptism with fire, the purging and abiding of the Holy Ghost. They cannot
condescend to think and walk in a realm
so low; they move about in an atmosphere of pride and self-conceit. They
propose by means of human culture to
lift themselves upon a plane of angelic
attainment and being; but worst of all,
they have set themselves to rob the
Church of its faith, to tear away the
foundations from beneath it, and to scat-
ter the children of God into a vast and
boundless wilderness of contradicting
philosophies and opinions where they can
find no rest for their souls.

One is reminded of a declaration by
Thomas Carlisle when, in his old age, he
wrote: "The soul of man still fights
against the dark influences of ignorance,
misery and sin, still lacerates itself like a
captive bird against the iron limits which
necessity has drawn around it; still fol-
lows false shadows, seeking peace and
good on paths where no peace, no good is
to be found." Thus it is, that those who

have turned away from the foundations which God has laid, grope in darkness, assail the faith, deceive the people, and wander into a wilderness where there is no cloud by day or pillar of fire by night to guide them; no sweet manna of spiritual food falling out of heaven to nourish and strengthen them.

The advocates of the new theology are especially prejudiced against Moses. They feel if they can prove that he did not write the Pentateuch, they have removed the heaviest stone from the foundation which supports the entire superstructure of Christian faith and hope.

A few decades ago the destructive critics claimed that the first five books of the Bible could not have been written by Moses because, at that time, the art of writing had not been discovered and developed to a stage that would have made it possible to produce these books. They felt perfectly safe and secure in their assertion that Moses did not write the Pentateuch because writing did not exist. The pick and spade of the archeologist have brought to light from the ruins of ancient civilizations and cities the fact that writing did exist in the days of Moses; that there was ample culture and methods for the production of these books. The enemies of the Mosaic authorship of the Scriptures then undertook to prove that Moses was not inspired from God to write these books, but that he gathered up the contents of these books from literature in existence; that it was more of a compilation than a revelation; that he was setting down, not the thought of God revealed to him by the Holy Spirit, but the thought of ancient sages, who in their wisdom had written into their laws the foundation truths contained in the Mosaic records.

The unearthing of ancient literature reveals the fact that the writings of the times of Moses are the merest jargon when compared with the majestic truths written down by this inspired servant of God, as contained in these five books which claim his authorship. The enemies of these old foundation books have not been able, and will not be able, to find anything written in tablets or carved in stone dating back to the times of Moses that will begin to compare with the great truths contained in the Pentateuch. There is a majesty of movement and a depth of power and wisdom in the thought and word of God that lifts it into a realm entirely beyond and above the thoughts and words of men.

The Bible is THE BOOK. Nothing came before it, nothing has come after it, and nothing will ever be produced by man that can be compared to it. It lifts itself up above all literature, like a mountain above the plain. We recognize, because of its majesty and power, the Word of God wherever we meet it in literature, or hear it in speech. The poet weaves the scripture into his verse; the essayist intersperses the Word of God into his composition; the statesman strengthens his argument by quoting scripture; the lawyer seeks to win his case by calling the attention of the jury to the words of Moses, of David, and of Paul. In all the realm of human literature we find quotations from the sacred Book, and everywhere it lifts itself up superior to its surroundings. It stands out in striking contrast with the mere words and thoughts of men. It is as a mounted officer riding conspicuously among the regiments of infantry.

Quotations from the Holy Scriptures do not need the quotation marks to distinguish them as borrowed by authors to give spice, strength and tone to their literature. This is singular. The words are the same; they are spelled with the same letters, but the thought is God's thought, infinitely above man's thought. The Bible stands out alone entirely above and beyond all other literature. It is the Word of God. It reveals to man his origin, his duty and his destiny. It points to him the return road to God, the path of peace and happiness. Its counsels are infinitely wise; its laws are absolutely just; its gospel is full of hope and mercy; its truths are bread to the hungry, water to the thirsty, health to the sick, and a lamp to the weary feet of the prodigal, seeking the portals of the Father's house.

The enemies of the Bible, the men who would destroy its authority, who would take away the faith of the people in its divine origin, and trustworthiness, are enemies of law and order, of peace and progress, of consolation, comfort and hope. The Word of God, as contained in the Holy Scriptures, furnishes the sure foundation upon which we build good character, the home, secure the sacredness of the marriage vow, the order of the family; upon which we build the Church, with all of its blessings and help for the souls of men; upon which we build the state and secure rights of property, sacredness and protection of life; upon which we erect the whole social superstructure, and out of which we gather up, construct, get stimulation, courage and conviction for everything that contributes to the progress of civilization and the uplift of the race.

Destroy these foundations and what can the righteous do? Break down the faith of the people in the Word of God and you destroy the basis upon which we do business; you break the sacredness of the marriage vow; you leave children without control or protection; the Church falls to pieces, society disintegrates, commerce perishes, the weeds grow between the cross-ties of your great railway systems, the sails of trade flap idly in the winds, and the wheels of progress are turned backward; everything worth while loses its charm; man becomes a beast, life is not worth living, hope has no anchorage within the vale, and the world becomes dead and desolate.

Give us the Bible. Preach to us its truths, confirm our faith in its holy teaching, make us to feel that it is the law, the will, the Word of God; that it reveals to us His gracious care, His compassionate love, His plans for our redemption; that in the beyond there is life and peace and blessing; that we must give an account in the day of judgment for our conduct here; that life is given to us and extended that we may make preparation for the life that is to come. Build society upon this firm foundation; saturate the minds and hearts of men with the holy truths of the sacred Scriptures; make them to feel the authority of this holy Book and property is safe, life is sacred, the marriage vow is kept inviolate, the home is happy, society is pure, the Church is spiritual and like an army with banners; the courts are just, the sick are visited, the hungry are fed, the poor are clothed, the song of gladness is heard throughout the land, industry is on every hand, the shuttle of commerce shoots to and fro with its thread of blessing and prosperity in the warp of all nations; men trust each other, keep their promises, meet their obligations; friendships spring up; there is friendly commerce, not only in material goods, but in thoughts and ideals, across the seas. Wars disappear, and the kingdom of God comes down into the hearts of men and manifests itself in lives of rectitude and holiness.

God's people must not for one moment give attention and credence to the false teachings that we can give up the Old Testament Scriptures and retain the New; that we can cast away Moses and keep Paul; that we can destroy the foundations and preserve the superstructure. Those who would rob us of the Bible have nothing to give us in its stead. We desire nothing from them. The Bible, as we have it, meets our wants, comforts our hearts, and gives us the promise of the life that now is and that which is to come.

We have fallen upon times when preachers of the gospel and the lay people everywhere must earnestly contend for the faith; they must refuse to be deceived by the high-sounding words and difficult sentences of the destructive critic, who would make us believe that the Scriptures are not inspired, and that to hold on to them and believe them is not essential to our salvation.

Let it be remembered that our Lord said, "I came not to destroy the law and the prophets, but to fulfill"; and He was careful in His teachings, by references and quotations, to set His seal of approval forever upon the Old Testament Scriptures. The ages may grow gray, the furnaces of the sun may burn into dark cinders, the stars may fall, the oceans dry up, and the planets cease to roll in their splendor and beauty, but God's throne is eternal, and the word of the Lord abideth forever. On this foundation we rest our faith, and our undaunted and triumphant hope reaches out into eternity.

THE CHRIST OF PROPHECY.

"And beginning at Moses and all the prophets, he expounded unto them in all the scriptures the things concerning himself."—Luke 24:27.

According to our chronology it was something more than four thousand years from the fall of Adam to the crucifixion of Christ; but from the time of that fatal fall in the Garden of Eden, to that tragic crucifixion on the hill of Calvary, there was strung all along the highway of human history a line of prophecy bringing to sinful men the promise of a Redeemer.

The first hint of hope to fallen man is given in the promise that "The seed of the woman should bruise the serpent's head." From Mount Moriah Abraham saw the day of Christ and was glad.

I think there are three facts that will be readily admitted by all devout students of the Scriptures. First, the ancient Hebrew prophets saw in their visions and

117

promised in their messages a coming Redeemer and King. The harmony of the predictions with reference to this coming Messiah is most remarkable. The casual reader will soon understand that the different prophets, living in various countries, and at periods of time wide apart, beheld afar, and spoke of the same Christ. There are no contradictions or disagreements among the prophets concerning the world's Messiah. Their combined drawings make a complete picture of the Christ. Unite their writings and you have the earthly history of our Lord long before He was born in Bethlehem.

Second, Jesus Christ claimed to be the promised Messiah. He spoke of Himself as the Redeemer of whom the prophets had spoken through the centuries. He never hesitated to identify Himself as the sent of God in fulfillment of the prophecies of the ancient seers of Israel. He held to this claim when He knew it meant crucifixion. He testified to the same after His resurrection. In His birth, His life, His teachings, His sufferings and humiliation, His death, with the incidents connected therewith, His burial in a rich man's tomb, and His resurrection, our Lord Jesus is fully identified as the Christ of prophecy.

Third, the writers of the gospels and epistles contained in the New Testament believed, without hesitation or question, in the inspiration of the prophets and the divine truthfulness of what they had spoken. They also believed that Jesus of Nazareth was the Christ spoken of by the prophets, and that in every essential particular He fulfilled all that they had said and written of Him.

We have here three witnesses of highest possible character and trustworthiness to the inspiration and infallibility of the Word of God in this perfect agreement of prophet, Christ, and apostles, all uniting in beautiful harmony around the identity and Deity of our crucified and risen Lord.

There is no more interesting or profitable study than to take the Old Testament writings concerning the coming, the life, the sufferings, and the final victory and glory of our Lord Jesus, and then to turn to the New Testament and, following the footsteps of the earthly life and ministry of our Lord, to notice how perfectly that life, with its sorrows and its blessings upon men, fits into the predictions contained in the prophecies of the Old Testament. There is no possible way to account for this perfect harmony and agreement except we acknowledge at once that the ancient prophets were inspired and that Christ is divine.

Of course, it must be understood that much prophecy contained in the Old Testament has no direct reference to Christ. In this wonderful book we find many prophecies concerning the growth, development, and prosperity of Israel. Here their backslidings are foretold, the fall of Jerusalem and the dispersion of the Jews are faithfully pointed out; their sufferings, wanderings, and scatterings through all the nations of the earth are foreseen, and their final restoration is promised. We also have prophecies concerning the fate that was to overtake great heathen cities and the punishment that would fall upon those nations who persecuted the Jews. These predictions have turned from prophecy into history; they have been fulfilled in so remarkable a way that honest and devout men can form no other conclusion than that the prophets who foresaw these coming events were inspired by the Holy Spirit. The remarkable fulfillment of prophecy with intelligent and honest men, lifts the Bible entirely out of the realm of possible guesswork or forgery and places it upon the firm foundation of divine inspiration.

The devout student of prophecy will only be able to rightly divide the word of truth when he recognizes the fact that one group of prophecies concerning Christ points to His first coming in humiliation to suffer for a lost race, and to set on foot a scheme of redemption and a gospel evangel to bring the race to repentance and saving faith; and that another group of prophecies points to His second coming in power and great glory to reign and rule over a redeemed people.

In the first coming of our Lord those splendid prophecies of His lordship, His reign and rule as King of kings and Lord

of lords, were not fulfilled; but the
prophecies concerning His humiliation
and suffering were so completely fulfilled in every detail we need have no
uneasiness with reference to those inspired promises which point to His
coming in power and glory. The fulfillment of the prophecies concerning His
humiliation, His sufferings and death has
been so accurate in every detail that they
offer a firm foundation upon which to
rest our faith that the day of His second
coming, glory, and victorious reign will
dawn with triumph. The Word of God,
through His inspired seers, has not failed
and cannot fail.

The text refers to a conversation which
took place between Jesus and two of His
disciples directly after His resurrection,
as they walked together up the road from
Jerusalem to Emmaus. We have often
wished that this conversation might have
been written down as it fell from the lips
of our Lord, and have found its place in
the New Testament. It will be remembered that the disciples were lamenting
the death of their Lord, and were quite

puzzled over some rumors they had heard with reference to His resurrection. Believing Jesus to be a stranger in the community they undertook to give Him some outline of the sad events which had occurred during the past few days. As Jesus saw how utterly they failed to comprehend Him and His mission He rebuked them for their "slowness of heart to believe all that the prophets had spoken. And beginning at Moses and all the prophets, he expounded unto them in all the scriptures the things concerning himself."

What a wonderful opening up and application of prophecy this must have been! I suppose He reminded them of that early promise that "The seed of the woman should bruise the serpent's head." No doubt, He called their attention to the words of Moses, "A prophet shall the Lord, your God, raise up unto you among your brethren like unto me; him shall ye hear." Perhaps He mentioned the lifting up of the brazen serpent in the wilderness for the healing of the bitten and sinful people. It may be He quoted where Job had said, "I know that my Redeemer liveth."

If in the conversation the disciples had referred to the cruelties heaped upon Jesus by those who crucified Him He could have quoted to them from the 22nd Psalm: "All they that see me laugh me to scorn: they shoot out the lip, they shake the head, saying, He trusted on the Lord that He would deliver Him: let Him deliver Him, seeing He delighteth in Him." He also might have mentioned to them in the same Psalm, "They parted my garments among them, and cast lots upon my vesture." He perhaps reminded them of a prophecy in Zech. 11: "And I said unto them, if ye think good, give me my price; and if not, forbear. So they weighed for my price thirty pieces of silver. And the Lord said unto me, Cast it unto the potter: a goodly price that I was prised at of them. And I took the thirty pieces of silver, and cast them to the potter in the house of the Lord."

Our Lord must have called their attention to that beautiful prophecy in Micah 5: "But thou, Bethlehem Ephratah, though thou be little among the thousands of Judah, yet out of thee shall he come forth unto me that is to be ruler in Israel: whose goings forth have been from of old, from everlasting." He could hardly have omitted calling their attention to Isaiah 53, which so vividly describes His humble person, His patient sufferings, and His cruel death. "He was despised and rejected of men; a man of sorrows, and acquainted with grief: and we hid as it were our faces from him. He was despised, and we esteemed him not. Surely he hath borne our griefs, and carried our sorrows: yet we did esteem him stricken, smitten of God, and afflicted. But he was wounded for our trangressions, he was bruised for our iniquities: the chastisement of our peace was upon him; and with his stripes we are healed. All we like sheep have gone astray; we have turned every one to his own way; and the Lord hath laid upon him the iniquity of us all." And so Isaiah goes forward centuries before the birth of Christ, giving in minute detail the incidents connected with His sufferings and death for the sins of the race.

Our Lord may have quoted from Isaiah 7:14: "Therefore the Lord himself shall give you a sign; Behold a virgin shall conceive, and bear a son, and shall call his name Immanuel." With reference to His resurrection He could have pointed them to that Psalm in which it is said, "For thou wilt not leave my soul in the grave, neither wilt thou suffer thine Holy One to see corruption." He could have referred them to the fact that way back in Psalm 22, the prophet poet of Israel had written the very words of His lamentation on the cross, "My God, my God, why hast thou forsaken me?" He could have pointed out in Zech. 9, a prophecy that they themselves had seen fulfilled, when He rode into Jerusalem, which was written centuries before His birth: "Rejoice greatly, O daughter of Zion; shout, O daughter of Jerusalem: behold thy King cometh unto thee; he is just, and having salvation; lowly, and riding upon an ass, and upon a colt the foal of an ass." Every

Bible reader will recall how literally this scripture was fulfilled.

In Exodus 12:46, in giving the law concerning sacrifices, the Hebrews were instructed that no bone of the passover lamb should be broken. David, referring to the Christ, says, "He keepeth all his bones: not one of them is broken." Turning to John 19:32, we read, "Then came the soldiers, and brake the legs of the first, and of the other which was crucified with him. But when they came to Jesus, and saw that he was dead already, they brake not his legs. But one of the soldiers with a spear pierced his side, and forthwith came there out blood and water. And he that saw it bare record, and his record is true; and he knoweth that he saith true, that ye might believe. For these things were done, that the scripture should be fulfilled, A bone of him shall not be broken." It is also said by the Psalmist, "They looked on him whom they pierced."

We readily recall the fact that when our Lord was found to be dead and the soldiers refrained from breaking His legs, they made sure of His death by driving a spear into His side and gazing upon Him as the blood and water trickled from His wound. And thus we have the most remarkable fulfillment of Scripture in the incidents which are connected with His crucifixion.

All of these prophecies, with their fulfillment, our Lord could have woven into His conversation with the disciples as they walked to Emmaus, "And beginning at Moses and all the prophets, he expounded unto them in all the scriptures the things concerning himself."

What a complete and perfect foundation the Old Testament Scriptures offer for the entire superstructure of the New Testament Scriptures, the Messiahship of Jesus Christ, His Godhead, the Christian Church, world evangelism, and the blessed hope of His second coming in glory and power to bring order out of chaos, peace out of war, plenty out of want, restful faith out of all doubts, and complete satisfaction to all the hunger and longing of the human soul.

We shall not listen to the arguments or

consent for one moment to those despoilers of the faith, who would have us give up the Old Testament, or turn away from the prophecies concerning our Lord contained therein. It is in this sacred Book that we are taught centuries before His coming into the world in the form of a man, that He was to be born of a virgin; that He was to be born in Bethlehem; that His enemies would seek to destroy His life in His infancy; that He was to be called up out of Egypt; that He was to bring a burning and shining light to apostate Israel; that to Him the Gentiles should seek; that He was to be betrayed by one of His followers; that thirty pieces of silver should be fixed as the price of His betrayal; that this same blood money should be used to purchase a potters' field; that He should ride into Jerusalem on an ass's colt; that He was to be made a prisoner; that His sacred back should be lashed with stripes; that His hands and feet should be pierced at His crucifixion; that He should suffer between malefactors; that none of His bones should be broken; that He should be pierced; that He should be buried in a rich man's grave, and that out of it all, and over it all, He should become gloriously triumphant — "See of the travail of his soul and be satisfied."

The Old Testament and the New are united in perfect and beautiful harmony, bound together inseparably in the life, the love, the death, and resurrection of our Lord Jesus. We rest our faith and peacefully trust the salvation of our immortal souls upon the truth of these scriptures, the identity of the Messiah, His deity and eternal Godhead, His power to save from sin, to sanctify our souls, and present us without spot or wrinkle to His Father in the presence of the holy hosts of heaven.

The Lord Jesus Christ in Old Testament and New is the answer of God to the deep longings of the human soul. The spirit of man created in the image and likeness of its Maker, cannot, will not, be content or satisfied with material things. It has appetites that cannot be satisfied with the things of time; it has a thirst that cannot be slaked with all the waters of

Niagara, a hunger that cannot be fed by the cattle upon a thousand hills. Wealth only increases its inertia and dissatisfaction. The things of this world, at their full, only remind us of its starving emptiness. The immortal soul of man has a hungering and thirsting that nothing in all the universe can feed and quench but God Himself.

Man was created for God, and God has mercifully implanted in him a cry that can only be hushed when the wandering child feels the embrace of the infinite arms of the eternal Father; a loneliness that can but long for the bread at the Father's house; a desolation that cannot find peace and rest until it finds it in companionship with Jesus. To find Jesus, to feel His love, to recognize His deity, to put one's past sins under His atoning blood, to realize the sanctifying and cleansing power of His holiness, inbreathed by the Holy Ghost, is to bring the soul into rest, consolation and comfort, contentment and praise. Jesus Christ is all and in all. Jesus Christ found, trusted in, realized in the forgiveness of sins, in the cleansing of the heart from all moral depravity and corruption, in the outpouring of His infinite love, is heaven. He is eternal life. To believe in Him in the fullness of His grace and power, and to rest one's trust in Him, is to have entered upon eternal life here without any fears or misgivings with regard to the hereafter.

Oh, immaculate Son of God! Oh, Saviour, sanctifier, keeper, thou satisfier and delight of the immortal souls of redeemed men, eternity will be too short to tell our love and ascribe our praise for Thee! Thou wast with the Father before the world was. Thy coming into the world was not the beginning of Thy existence. Thou didst never know sin; temptations were hurled at Thee in vain. In the glory of Thy Godhead thou didst understand Satan and all of his wiles and was infinitely beyond his reach. Thou didst live in the midst of poverty and taste the sorrows of the poor. Thou didst walk and labor with the ignorant and pity their stupidity. Thou didst receive sinners, eat with them, and look with compassion upon their wickedness. Thou didst weep with sorrowing men, and forgive the sinful, but thou wast God, eternal, pre-existent. Thou wast present when the morning stars sang together, and the sons of God shouted for joy. Thou art the same, yesterday, today, and forever.

Thou wilt come again. We wait for Thee. Years cannot wear out our patience, centuries hinder our longing, or millenniums dim our hope, or hush the joyful song in our souls, as we contemplate Thy coming in Thy glory, when we shall behold Thee King of kings and Lord of lords, and with prophet, priest, apostles and the saints of the ages, worship Thee in the full content of our raptured and immortal spirits through all eternity. Amen.

www.ingramcontent.com/pod-product-compliance
Lightning Source LLC
Chambersburg PA
CBHW020508040426
42331CB00042BA/100